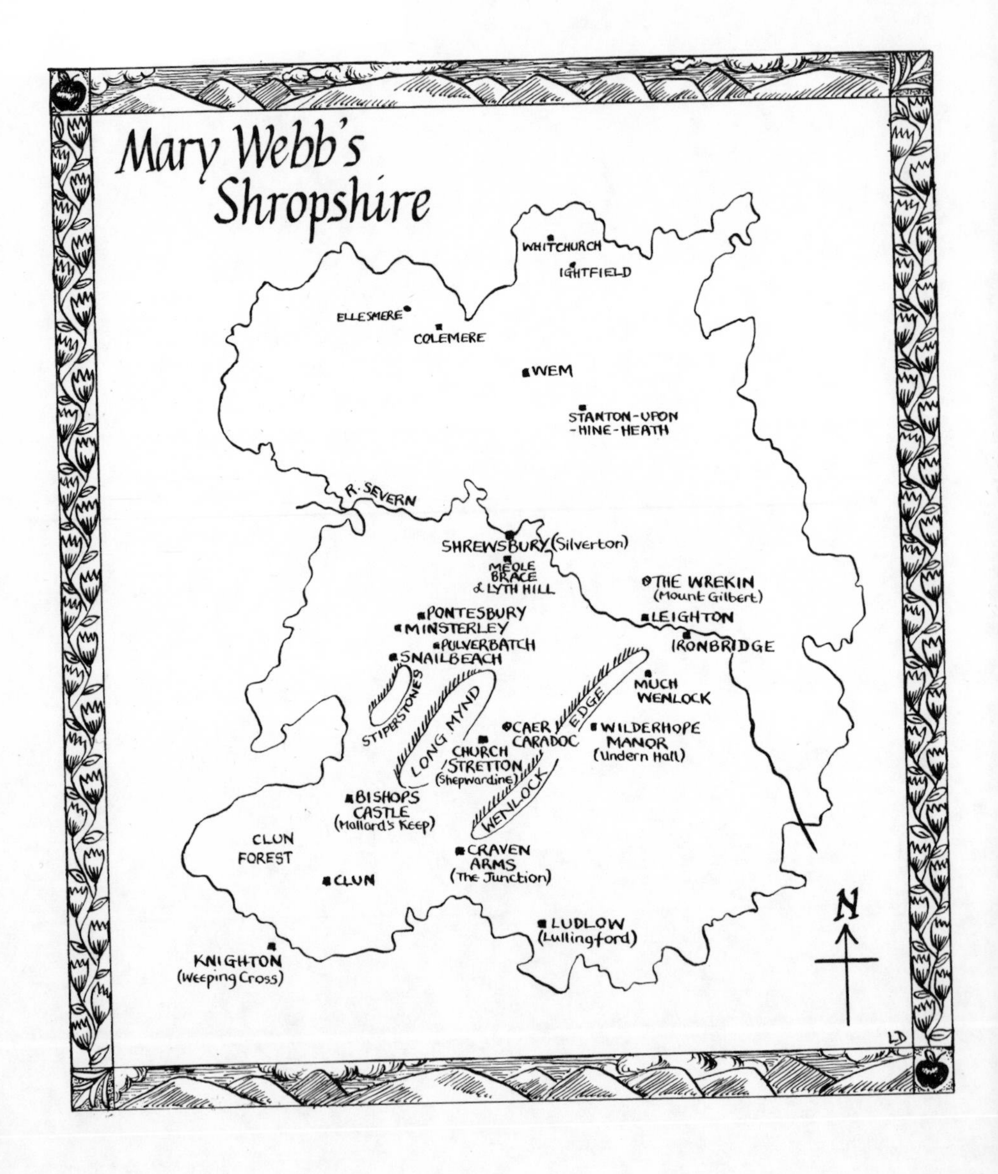

Mary Webb's Shropshire
WHITCHURCH
IGHTFIELD
ELLESMERE
COLEMERE
WEM
STANTON-UPON
-HINE-HEATH
R. SEVERN
SHREWSBURY (Silverton)
MEOLE
BRACE
& LYTH HILL
THE WREKIN
(Mount Gilbert)
LEIGHTON
IRONBRIDGE
PONTESBURY
MINSTERLEY
PULVERBATCH
SNAILBEACH
STIPERSTONES
LONG MYND
MUCH
WENLOCK
CAER
CARADOC
EDGE
WILDERHOPE
MANOR
(Undern Hall)
CHURCH
STRETTON
(Shepwardine)
WENLOCK
BISHOPS
CASTLE
(Mallard's Keep)
CLUN
FOREST
CLUN
CRAVEN
ARMS
(The Junction)
LUDLOW
(Lullingford)
KNIGHTON
(Weeping Cross)
N
LD

MARY WEBB COUNTRY

AN INTRODUCTION TO HER LIFE AND WORK

Compiled by

LINDA DAVIES

Published by
Palmers Press, 5 Castle Street, Ludlow
and Printed by
Orphans Press Ltd., Hereford Road, Leominster.

Cover Photograph: Ludlow (Lullingford) from Tinkers Hill by Jeremy Hall

ISBN 1 870054 03 2

In English Literature there is a tradition of regional writers, that is, writers strongly associated with a particular county, region or landscape. These include Thomas Hardy and Wessex, Emily Bronte and the Yorkshire Moors, Daphne du Maurier and Cornwall and D. H. Lawrence and the Industrial Midlands. Not all regional writers necessarily write exclusively about their particular landscape, or even spend much time there, but they have chosen to capture and portray a unique essence of place, whether it be natural or man-made.

This ability to bring a region or area of countryside to life may spring from a deep affection for it, from intimate knowledge of it or even possibly, from intense dislike of it. Whatever the motive, the result is that the writer becomes forever synonymous in the minds of his readers, with a place he has made his own.

One such writer is Mary Webb. Her picture of Shropshire is composed from her intense love of the county and her minutely detailed knowledge of its geography and natural history.

In her novels, the landscape of Shropshire profoundly affects those who live within it and those who make their living from it. It inspires intense feelings in her characters and some can be said to identify themselves with it in a deeply mystical way - difficult to explain in rational terms. Indeed it is impossible to imagine some - for example Hazel Woodus or Robert Rideout surviving elsewhere, just as Mary Webb herself wilted and sickened when she was away.

She wrote: "The hero of a country story must be instinct with the countryside: it is in his very bones. So it must always be in a novel that attempts the interpretation of earth through character. For the dwellers in mountain and forest are under this burden, that they must unconsciously express those dumb masses and forces that have no other voice than theirs. No novel of the countryside can attain greatness unless it unifies its characters with the earth, half frustrate, half triumphal."

And of Shropshire in particular she wrote: "Shropshire is a county where the dignity and beauty of ancient things lingers long, and I have been fortunate ... in being born and brought up in its magical atmosphere."

Although Mary Webb was a poet and a poetic novelist, she combined her vision with exceedingly detailed observations of nature, which serve to anchor her work in a real landscape - a landscape which is still recognisable today. She weaves her acutely observed descriptions of the land in all its moods, with the lives and actions of her characters. Thus are they not only sprung from the soil of Shropshire, but inseparable from it, just as she felt herself to be.

Thomas Moult, one of Mary Webb's earliest biographers wrote: "She has the love of earth epitomized in one special corner of earth."

And in his introduction to "Seven for a Secret" Robert Lynd wrote: "If it is necessary to classify novelists ... Mary Webb must be in a class that contains writers so different as Emily Bronte and Thomas Hardy, for whom the earth is predominantly a mystery - haunted landscape inhabited by mortals who suffer."

This book is not intended to be a critical analysis. My aim is to provide a brief biography of Mary Webb and an introduction to her writing, with numerous extracts to illustrate her portrayal of the landscape and natural history of Shropshire and its deep effect on her characters. The commentary is mine but otherwise I have endeavoured, as far as possible, to allow Mary Webb's own words to speak for her.

* * * * * * * * * * *

Mary Webb was born Gladys Mary Meredith, on March 25th 1881, at Leighton Lodge. Leighton is a village about ten miles from Shrewsbury, on the road to Ironbridge. Leighton Hall, to which the Lodge belongs, was built in 1778, of red brick, and commands views of Wenlock Edge and the Stretton Hills. The village itself lies in a deep valley near the river Severn. Leighton Lodge can still be seen today, a three storey house, standing among trees in the grounds of the Hall.

Mary was christened at the nearby church of St. Mary. Her father George Edward was a teacher and her mother Sarah Alice, claimed to be related to Sir Walter Scott. Mary had five younger brothers and sisters - Kenneth, Douglas, Muriel, Olive and Mervyn. It was to prove significant that there was a seven year gap between Mary and her nearest sibling, Kenneth.

When Mary was one, the family moved to Much Wenlock, to a large house called The Grange, where Mary spent most of her childhood. The Grange was a Georgian house with a long drive and huge garden, on the edge of open meadowland.

During her time at Much Wenlock Mary went for frequent rides in the surrounding countryside with her father, with whom she had a close, loving relationship. George Meredith painted and wrote poetry and seems to have been a kind and humourous companion to the young Mary. From her trips and from conversation with her father, Mary acquired a great deal of knowledge about local places and habits and seems also to have inherited his deep love of the countryside.

Of Much Wenlock she wrote that it was: "a very Rip Van Winkle of a borough" that had fallen asleep somewhere in the Middle Ages "and if you should wonder at the fashion of its garments, you must remember that it had not, since the day it fell asleep, changed its coat, its hosen or its hat".

Mary's relationship with her mother is less clear-cut. Moult described Alice Webb as nobleminded with a strong sense of duty, justice and honour, while Dorothy P. H. Wrenn described her as "unamiable, cold and selfish", indifferent towards her children and "resentful of her belated maternity".

It seems to be true that she never settled at The Grange and, after a riding accident, she became a permanent invalid, some sources stating that she shut herself away and virtually ignored her husband and children. Certainly the care of her younger brothers and sisters fell to Mary, causing her stress which led to the first breakdown in her health, when she was twenty.

When Mary was ten, a governess, Miss E. M. Lory joined the family. She encouraged Mary in her efforts to write and became Minoni, a lifelong friend. Mary was sent away to school in Southport for a short time when she was about fourteen but returned home to take care of the family - playing with the children and writing stories for them. During her brief time at school Mary did well, winning a prize for French.

In 1896, after her return home, George Meredith retired from teaching and the family moved again, to Stanton-on-Hine Heath, about five miles south-east of Wem and about six miles north of Shrewsbury. Their new home was a large red brick house, The Woodlands which was later renamed Hawkstone Park. While living here Mary began to write for the parish magazine - her first published work.

For some reason her mother Alice suddenly decided to return to normal life and took over the running of the household once more. Although relieved of the burden of responsibility for her brothers and sisters, the change does not seem to have been beneficial for Mary. She began to shut herself away in her bedroom to read and write while, at the same time suffering weight loss and fatigue.

Her illness developed into Graves Disease, from which she suffered for the rest of her life and which, partially at least, caused her premature death.

Graves Disease is an excess of thyroxine in the thyroid gland, which leads to over-activity, excessive perspiration and a rapid pulse. Sufferers eat large quantities of food to replace wasted energy but remain thin, with bulging, staring eyes. An ugly goitre on the neck was another side-effect suffered by Mary and she began to wear high-necked dresses to hide it.

While she was still recuperating from the first attack of Graves Disease, the family moved again, to Meole Brace on the outskirts of Shrewsbury. Mary was twenty-one. Their new house, smaller than those they had left, was called Maesbrook, and Mary lived there until her marriage when she was thirty.

She was writing essays and poems at this stage and was greatly influenced by Housman's nature poetry and by Shakespeare. She discussed Darwin's "Origin of the Species" with one of her brothers who later wrote: "The result of all this proved to be a pagan one. Her God was Nature".

* * * * * * * * * * *

Hazel Buds

Now breaks the sheath and spreads the leaf!
The bank beneath, the branch above,
Are set with nests, are homes of love.
So goodbye, grief!

With restful haste and gentle strife
Pink hazel stipules are unfurled,
Pink dawns are flung across the world.
So welcome, life!

* * * * * * * * * * *

A collection of twelve of Mary's essays was published in 1917 but was written much earlier. These essays show an acute observation of nature, and outlined her belief that God's being is revealed to us in natural beauty. Of beauty itself she wrote: "...the thought - so dim and so dear - that all fine contours are a direct message from God, is rooted deep in the minds of the simple-hearted, who are the Magi of the world."

And: "...when the church has crumbled with its dogma, the ivy covers all with its kindly curtain and speaks of a life greater than these..."

She referred to "the complex life of nature which is the life of God".

Of her essays "The Spring of Joy", Walter de la Mare wrote: "Few observers have taken the pains to describe an object so minute in terms so precise, yet the words are poetic in effect: they are charged with life and significance, and only a loving rapture in the thing itself could have found them for this purpose."

MARY AS A GIRL

In January 1909 Mary's father died. He was buried in a churchyard at Ightfield near Whitchurch on the northern border of Shropshire. Mary was distraught and took refuge once more in writing poetry. Her distress brought about a recurrence of her illness and she was an invalid for some time after her father's death.

* * * * * * * * * * *

Alder Buds

On New Year's Day I set beside his bed
An alder branch, already bravely budded.
He smiled, but hardly cared to turn his head
And see how close the purple spheres were studded,
Wherein the April leaves lay slumbering.
He spoke of leaves that rustled by his pillows,
More golden-sweet than airs in summer willows.
I did not know he would not see the spring.

* * * * * * * * * * *

Two years later, in January 1911, Mary attended a literary gathering in Meole Brace and there she was introduced to her future husband, Henry Webb, a man five years her junior. He was a Cambridge graduate and schoolteacher whose abstracted gentleness possibly reminded Mary of her father. In addition they shared an interest in writing and a love of the countryside and, understandably, their relationship flourished. (Henry Webb wrote a trilogy of novels about thirteenth century France under the pseudonym J. Clayton.)

Mary and Henry were married in Meole Brace Parish Church in 1912 and spent their honeymoon in the countryside near Church Stretton.

After their honeymoon they left Shropshire and settled in Weston-super-Mare where Henry was to teach for the next two years. Mary was unhappy there and began to realise that she would never be able to live away from her beloved Shropshire. It was during this period of exile that she began work on her first novel "The Golden Arrow".

Eventually Henry resigned and the Webbs returned to Shropshire, to Rose Cottage, a small house with a large garden, just outside Pontesbury, ten miles south west of Shrewsbury. Here Mary gathered together all the notes she had made and began to write. She wrote so quickly that Henry had to buy her a special fast-flowing fountain pen! and "The Golden Arrow" was completed in just three weeks.

* * * * * * * * * * *

We have sought it, we have sought the golden arrow
(Bright the sally-willows sway)
Two and two by paths low and narrow,
Arm-in-crook along the mountain way.

Break o' frost and break o' day!
Some were sobbing through the gloom
When we found it, when we found the golden arrow -
Wand of willow in the secret cwm.

"The Golden Arrow" is based on an old Shropshire legend which says that the Golden Arrow of Pontesford Hill will bring good luck to any lovers who find it on Palm Sunday. It is set in the Shropshire hill country in the south west corner of the county - the Stiperstones and the Devil's Chair which broods, an ominous presence throughout the novel.

The Stiperstones stretch five miles, from Wood End to Minsterley. The Devil's Chair, which is about half-way along, is a mass of glacial rock which rises about one hundred feet above the range. Legend has it that no person may sit in the Chair without having bad luck unless they have sought and found the Golden Arrow - symbol of unselfish love. It is said that when the Chair is shrouded in mist, the Devil is sitting in it.

"The Golden Arrow" opens with a description of the cottage which is the home of the Arden family, and the hilly landscape around it.

"John Arden's stone cottage stood in the midst of the hill plateau, higher than the streams began, shelterless to the four winds. While washing dishes Deborah could see, through the small, age-misted pane, counties and blue ranges lying beneath the transparent or hazy air in the bright, unfading beauty of inviolate nature. She would gaze out between the low window-frame and the lank geraniums, forgetting the half-dried china, when grey rainstorms raced across from far Cader Idris, ignoring in their majestic progress the humble, variegated plains of grass and grain, breaking like a tide on the unyielding heather and the staunch cottage."

The sensitive, spiritual Deborah Arden falls in love with Stephen Southernwood, foreman of the nearby Lostwithin Mine. Because he is unequal to the relationship, he abandons Deborah and their unborn child. Deborah survives her devastation at his betrayal and, when he returns repentant, they are able to resume their life together in greater understanding and strength

Stephen has learned that a relationship must have a spiritual as well as a physical side and, with this new-found wisdom, it seems more likely that they will be able to withstand the threat of the Devil's Chair which has exerted a malign influence over their marriage from the start.

In fact the Devil's Chair is such an intrusive presence throughout the novel that it is almost a character in its own right.

"On the highest point of the bare, opposite ridge, now curtained in driving storm-cloud, towered in gigantic aloofness a mass of quartzite, blackened and hardened by uncountable ages... The scattered rocks, the ragged holly-brakes on the lower slopes were like small carved lions beside the black marble steps of a stupendous throne. Nothing ever altered its look... It remained inviolable, taciturn, evil. It glowered darkly on the dawn; it came through the snow like jagged bones through flesh; before its hardness even the venturesome cranberries were discouraged. For miles around, in the plains, the valleys, the mountain dwellings it was feared."

"The Devil's Chair loomed over them - for all the distance between - like a fist flourished in the face. It was dark as purple nightshade."

In all of Mary Webb's novels there are characters sensitive to the landscape, almost rooted in it, so that its moods affect them deeply. It is apparent early in "The Golden Arrow" that Deborah is such a person - in contrast with the shallow, unthinking Lily, who marries Deborah's brother Joe.

"Deborah was looking at a giant shadow - the astral body of the gaunt Diafol ridge, blue-purple as a flower of hound's-tongue - which stretched across the hammock-like valley towards their own range at this time in the afternoon.

'Aye', she said absently.

'Do you like these sausage-curls at the back Deb?' asked Lily, thirsty for female praise, since the more nerve-thrilling male was not obtainable.

'Aye,' said Deborah again.

Lily stamped.

'You never looked Deborah Arden! I suppose you're jealous.'

Deborah awakened from her dreams and smiled.

'I was thinking that shadow was like a finger pointing straight at you and me Lil,' she said. 'A long finger as you canna get away from. What does it token?'

'Weddings!' said Lily...''

By loving Stephen, Deborah has found the Golden Arrow about which John, her father tells them after Stephen has asked her to live with him. Later in the novel Deborah says:

''Seems to me, loving's like the Golden Arrow - bright and sharp, and him that finds it'll keep it against the 'orld. There's not a many do find it.''

And, initially the couple are at odds because Stephen has not found the Arrow and does not find it until he leaves and returns, to initial rejection by Deborah.

But, unaware of what lies ahead, including Stephen's inadequacy, Deborah promises to be his sweetheart.

''They had come to the point where emotions are crude and huge - like a naked land of beetling rock. They reached the place of Deborah's morning promise - Joe and Lily were ahead. Deborah looked up and smiled, forgetting in her joy the pain that went with it. 'It's the secret cwm,' she said, 'where the arrow was!'''

Deborah and Stephen set up home together, although he will not marry her. Their cottage is beneath the shadow of the Devil's Chair, and from the start it casts a blight upon their doomed relationship. Even when Stephen finally does ask Deborah to marry him and she accepts with joy, there is no answering joy in the surrounding landscape.

''Outside, the Chair reared itself haughtily above the cowering land. Around it, as the August night drove on, and the mists stood in the plain to the tops of twenty-foot hedges like water in deep bowls, rose and moved in silence impalpable tenebrae. They swept round it as if in a dark incantation, with beckoning arms and stealthy haste, passing across the dim waste of burnt heather in lost eddies.''

And on her wedding day the wind rages and the land appears wild and unforgiving. There are no good omens for Deborah's happiness.

Symbolically also, summer is over, and the drabness of autumn in the countryside around the cottage depresses Stephen.

"He was thinking how dull the country was getting, how forlorn. For the colours were withdrawing with what seemed to him the terrible leisureliness of fatality. They would soon be gone as the willow-wrens were gone from the woods below Lostwithin, as the cuckoos had long been gone from field and hill. The density was gone from the shadows, scent dwindled daily, the stars were like scimitars instead of silver flowers."

He begins to hate the countryside and long to be back in town.

"The woods that he went through on his way to work grew spectral, cold mist swirled there; dead leaves hung on the boughs like rows of weasels and magpies before a keeper's house. A cold presence moved among the sad perspectives of the larch and oak boles; sinister, inimical to joy, the Dark Keeper went his rounds - strangling life, hanging the shrivelled corpse of beauty in the bleak air derisively."

"He wished more and more as September slipped by that he had never taken the cottage. The whole countryside was acquiring in his eyes something portentous, apocalyptic."

His depression increases until he finally begins to doubt the existence of God or indeed of any reason for living. His horror at the emptiness suddenly revealed to him, is symbolised by the Devil's Chair.

"- an empty throne. There it was; no devil, no angel, no god ever was there, ever would be, nothing... He shuddered at the appalling picture. He could not get the look of the empty throne of black rock from his mind."

Eventually he makes a futile attempt to destroy the Chair with explosives but fails even to damage it.

"The Chair looked exactly as it had always done. He could not detect even a nick in it from this distance. All his trouble had not altered it in the least."

Stephen has neither the strength of character to endure his situation, nor the shallowness to be indifferent to it, and so it is inevitable that he will leave. Deborah, half-demented at his desertion, goes home to her parents and bears his child alone. When spring comes, although broken by his betrayal, she takes the baby out into the countryside and, gazing at the distant Devil's Chair, she begins to find a kind of spiritual peace through acceptance.

At this moment Stephen returns, a changed man and, suffering first her rejection, finds at last, the Golden Arrow.

"He knew that now neither the wilderness nor dark weather, devils, nor the infinite void, mattered to him in the least. His love for Deborah made him impregnable to terror, gave him a grasp of truth deeper than reason. He had found the golden arrow, to his own agony and ennobling."

* * * * * * * * * * *

During their time at Rose Cottage the Webbs decided to supplement their income by selling flowers and fruit from their garden in Shrewsbury Market. They were living chiefly on the small annual allowance made to Mary by her mother, now living in Chester. Henry was suffering from ill-health and earning only a small amount from private coaching.

Rose Cottage, Pontesbury

It was Mary who walked the nine miles to Shrewsbury every week, to sell produce. At first she supplied other stall-holders but then took a stall for herself. Henry stayed at home and sold apples near to Rose Cottage.

The weekly trips to market do not seem to have been a hardship to Mary. She loved the long walk through the Shropshire countryside and then the bustle and colour of the market. But such an activity certainly lowered her in the estimation of her neighbours who regarded the couple as strange.

* * * * * * * * * * *

The Happy Life

No silks have I, no furs nor feathers,
But one old gown that knows all weathers;
No veils nor parasols nor lace,
But rough hands and a tanned face.
Yet the soft, crinkled leaves are mine
Where pale, mysterious veins shine,
And laced larches upon the blue,
And grey veils where the moon looks through;
The cries of birds across the lawns
In dark and teeming April dawns;
The sound of wings at the door-sill,
Where grows the wet-eyed tormentil;
The ripe berry's witcheries -
Its perfect round that satisfies;
And the gay scent of the wood I burn,
And the slap of butter in a busy churn.

* * * * * * * * * * *

Eventually the rent for Rose Cottage proved to be too great a burden and in 1916 the Webbs moved a mile from Pontesbury, to The Nills, which had a lower rent. This cottage, on the slopes of the Stiperstones, was very remote, down a rough track which forded a stream. The cottage itself was hidden from view by trees.

When they moved Mary gave up her trips to market and their financial position grew even worse. Henry had to take a teaching post in Chester which meant that, during the summer of 1916 they were only able to return to The Nills at weekends.

Mary was depressed at living away from Shropshire - feeling that she had no place in the city. She was also deeply affected by the First World War - all three brothers, Kenneth, Douglas and Mervyn were overseas as soldiers and her sister Muriel was in Gibraltar. Mervyn was injured, which must have added to her misery and her conviction that only by turning to nature could man hope to put an end to war.

* * * * * * * * * * *

The Lad Out There

Oh, Powers of Love, if still you lean
Above a world so black with hate,
Where yet - as it has ever been -
The loving heart is desolate,
Look down upon the lad I love,
(My brave lad, tramping through the mire) -
Light Thou the stars for him above!
Now nights are dark and mornings dim,
Let him in his long watching know
That I too count the minutes slow
And light the lamp of love for him.
The sight of death, the sleep forlorn,
The old homesickness vast and dumb -
Amid these things, so bravely borne,
Let my long thoughts about him come.
I see him in the weary file;
So young he is, so dear to me,
With ever ready sympathy
And wistful eyes and cheerful smile.
However far he travels on,
Thought follows, like the willow-wren
That flies the stormy seas again
To lands where her delight is gone.
Whatever he may be or do
While absent far beyond my call,
Bring him, the long day's march being through,
Safe home to me some evenfall!

* * * * * * * * * * *

Mary felt so out of place in the city that she was unable to write. Even the publication of "The Golden Arrow" does not seem to have encouraged her, although she had begun work on her second novel. So it was that "Gone to Earth" was written during those precious weekends at The Nills when Mary was, however briefly, back on Shropshire soil.

* * * * * * * * * * *

"Gone to Earth", written and published while the Great War was at its height, can be seen almost as an effigy of all the millions of young men who had "gone to earth". It is an anguished protest against cruelty and the evils which cruelty produces.

It is set in almost the same area of Shropshire as "The Golden Arrow" and its heroine, the tragic young woman Hazel Woodus, is the mouthpiece for Mary's abhorrence of cruelty and injustice. In spite of all that befalls her during the course of the novel, Hazel Woodus retains her essential innocence. She is doomed to suffer through her compassion and pity for the wild creatures which daily fall victim to man's cruelty.

Her love of wild creatures centres on her pet fox and, at the end of the novel, she dies in the attempt to save her from the hunt - a sacrifice reminiscent of Christ on the Cross or of the brave men who gave their lives in the War.

In almost the opening scene, Hazel and Foxy are described, bathed in the red light of the setting sun - a forward echo of the red blood of their coming martyrdom.

"The red light from the west stained her torn old dress, her thin face, her eyes, till she seemed to be dipped in blood. The fox, wistfulness in her expression and the consciousness of coming supper in her mind, gazed obediently where her mistress gazed, and was touched with the same fierce beauty. They stood there fronting the crimson pools over the far hills, two small sentient things facing destiny with pathetic courage; they had, in the chill evening on the lonely hill, a look as of those predestined to grief, almost an air of martyrdom."

As in "The Golden Arrow", landscape dominates the lives of Mary Webb's characters. The motherless Hazel lives with her negligent father in a cottage at the Callow (actually Callow Hill) - "a spinney of silver birches and larches that topped a round hill."

Five miles away is a hill called God's Little Mountain, based on Lordshill, which "towered ... darkly to the eastward," and which is where Hazel and Foxy finally meet their untimely end.

The land abounds with legends - none more powerful or frightening to Hazel than that of the death pack which brings doom to anyone who hears it give tongue.

"This was the legend and Hazel believed it implicitly. When she had found Foxy half dead outside her deserted earth, she had been quite sure that it was the death pack that had made away with Foxy's mother. She connected it also with her own mother's death. Hounds symbolized everything she hated, everything that was not young, wild and happy. She identified herself with Foxy, and so with all things hunted and shared and destroyed."

The two men who compete for Hazel represent the opposing physical and spiritual sides of her nature. She marries the parson Edward Marston who so respects her innocence that he makes no attempt to consummate the marriage. She is seduced by Jack Reddin, squire of Undern Hall.

Undern Hall, based on the real Wilderhope Manor, is a strange, sinister house, "crouched under its hill like a toad", inhabited only by Reddin and his warped manservant Andrew Vessons, who is tied to the place with "ties deep as the tangled roots of the bindweed".

It is a place that holds by hate instead of love and, in her description, Mary Webb hints at the effect the house has on those who live in it.

"Undern Hall, with its many small-paned windows, faced the north sullenly. It was a place of which the influence and magic were not good. Even in May, when the lilacs frothed into purple, paved the lawn with shadows, steeped the air with scent; ... still, something that haunted the place set the heart fluttering. No place is its own, and that which is most stained with old tumults has the strongest fascination."

Reddin awakens physical passion in Hazel with his ruthless and violent courting, while exuding that very cruelty which she detests. One of his few occupations is foxhunting, while Hazel cannot even bear to hear of an animal suffering.

"She, in her inexpressive, childish way, shared with the love-martyr of Galilee the heartrending capacity for imaginative sympathy."

Yet she is so naive that she begins to view Undern as a possible refuge for Foxy when her father threatens to drown the animal for stealing chickens.

Between God's Little Mountain and Undern is a conical hill called Hunter's Spinney.

"It was deeply wooded; only its top was bare and caught the light redly. It was a silent and deserted place, cowled in ancient legends. Here the Black Huntsman stalled his steed, and the death-pack coming to its precincts, ceased into the hill. Here, in November twilights, when the dumb birds cowered in the dark pines, you might hear from the summit a horn blown very clearly, with tuneful devilry, and a scattered sound of deep barking like the noise of sawing timber, and then the blood-curdling tumult of the pack at feeding time."

Here Hazel tells Edward Marston that she will marry the first man who asks her, in order to escape from her father and his threats to Foxy. And here Edward resolves to ask for her hand.

While Edward is suffering sleepless nights for fear that someone else will ask for Hazel first, he leaves his bed and goes out into the night.

"He saw the ice slip from the bright pointed lilac buds, and sheep browsing the frosty grass, and going to and fro in the unreserved way that animals have in the early hours before the restraint of human society is imposed on them. He saw, yet noticed nothing, until a long scarlet bar of cloud reminded him of Hazel by its vividness, and he found a violet by the grave-yard gate."

Hazel accepts Edward, to the great distress of his mother.

"'She's not a Christian, my dear,' said Mrs Marston in a kind of gasp, 'she refuses to be died for!'

Upstairs Hazel was saying her orisons at the window.

'If there's anybody there,' she murmured, staring out into the consuming darkness that had absorbed every colour, every form, except the looming outline of God's Little Mountain against a watery moon-rise - 'if there's anybody there I'd be obleeged if you'd give an eye to our Foxy, as is lonesome in tub. It dunna matter about me, being under Ed'ard's roof.'"

Hazel, Edward and her father attend an agricultural show where Hazel meets Jack Reddin who has been searching for her ever since their first meeting. She agrees to speak with him alone, and waits for him out in the dark.

"The hills loomed in the dusk over the show-ground. They were of a cold and terrific colour, neither purple nor black nor grey, but partaking of all. Kingly, mournful, threatening, they dominated the life below as the race dominates the individual."

The awfulness of the landscape makes Hazel homesick for the Callow. Life with Edward will be too righteous and the thought of Undern frightens her even more. She rejects Reddin, thus fuelling his passion for her, and marries Edward.

Unlike Deborah Arden's wedding, Hazel's is smiled upon by nature.

"The stately May morning, caparisoned in diamonds, full of the solemnity that perfect beauty wears, had come out of the purple mist and shamed the hovel where Hazel dressed for her bridal."

"The may-tree by the gate knew its perfect moment, covered with crystal buds that shone like rain among the bright green leaves. From every pear-tree - full-blossomed, dropping petals - and from every shell-pink apple-tree came the roar of the bees."

But it is not long before Reddin continues his relentless pursuit. He haunts the woods on God's Little Mountain, watching Hazel's movements and awaiting the opportunity to catch her alone. These woods are full of hidden life forces.

"These thick woods, remote on their ridges, were to the watchful eye rich with a half-revealed secret, to the attentive ear full of urgent voices... In this hour or in the next, from a grey ash-bole or a blood-red pine-trunk, might come the naked spirit of life with a face fierce or lovely... Reddin, not having a watchful eye or an attentive ear for such things, was not conscious of anything but a sense of loneliness."

When he does manage to speak with Hazel, she rejects him again, saying that he has blood on him because of the animals he kills. But at the same time she cannot help being fascinated by him and does not refuse outright to meet him again.

Hazel goes out early one morning to pick mushrooms and, on the way, she stops to speak to Foxy in the grave-yard. Here is the nearest Mary Webb, or perhaps anyone, can come to conveying in words the peculiar chemistry which can exist between animals and sensitive people.

''They held a long conversation, Hazel whispering, Foxy eloquent of eye. Foxy had a marked personality... She was possessed of herself: the wild was her kingdom. If she was in a kennel - so her expression led you to understand - she was there incognito and of her own choice. Hazel, sitting at Edward's table, had the same look.''

There follows a long, detailed description of the countryside around God's Little Mountain and Hazel's reaction to it - her joy and her feeling of being at one with the land.

''She had so deep a kinship with the trees, so intuitive a sympathy with leaf and flower, that it seemed as if the blood in her veins was not slow-moving human blood, but volatile sap.''

''Hazel, in the fields and woods, enjoyed it all so much that she walked in a mystical exaltation.''

Reddin, also abroad in the fields, is different.

''Reddin in the fields and woods enjoyed himself only. For he took his own atmosphere with him wherever he went, and before his footsteps weakness fled and beauty folded.''

His cruelty is emphasised later, in a second encounter.

''Suddenly a shout rang across the hill and silenced her and the woodlarks. She saw against the full-blown flower of the west - black on scarlet - Reddin on his tall black horse, galloping towards her. Clouds were coming up for night. They raced with him... Reddin came on, and the thunder of his horse's hoofs was in her ears. Hurtling thus over the pastures ... he was the embodiment of the destructive principle, of cruelty...''

Thus he smashes his way into Hazel's quiet communion with nature.

''Hazel ate the fairy tulips as a pixie might, sharp-toothed, often consuming them whole. So she partook of her sacrament in both kinds, and she partook of it alone, taking her wafers and her honeyed wine from hands she never saw, in a presence she could not gauge.''

Inevitably Reddin proves too strong for Hazel's resolve and she goes to meet him at Hunter's Spinney, knowing that she is taking an irrevocable step, but unable to stop herself.

''When she came to the beginning of Hunter's Spinney she felt frightened; the woods were so far-reaching, so deep with shadow; the trees made so sad a rumour, and swayed with such forlorn abandon. In the dusky places the hyacinths, broken but not yet faded, made a purple carpet, solemn as a pall.''

Reddin comes from Undern to claim her and, after he has virtually raped her:

''So they sat beneath the black, slow-moving branches under the threat of the oncoming night, weeping like children. They cowered, it seemed, beneath a hand raised to strike. All that they did was wrong; all that they did was inevitable...

''Some Being, it seemed, was listening there, and not only listening, but imposing in an effortless but inevitable way its veiled purpose.''

They are helpless victims of a force beyond their control and understanding - the spirit of the land.

From this moment Hazel is torn between the two men, loving Edward but feeling that she now belongs to Reddin. She suffers, the innocent victim of passion, no longer able to exist with either of them. Although she goes to Undern with Reddin, the house will never accept her, or be a place of happiness.

''She looked across at Undern. There were roses everywhere, but the house had so strong a faculty for imposing its personality that it gave to the red roses and the masses of traveller's joy that frothed over it a deep sadness, as if they had blown and dropped long since and were but memorial flowers.''

Significantly, she no longer sees it as a refuge for Foxy.

''Sometimes she was very homesick for Foxy, but she would not have her at Undern. She did not trust the place.''

Finally Hazel is forced to return to Edward. She cannot bear to live with Reddin in his careless cruelty. Although Edward takes her back and is prepared to care for Reddin's child, which Hazel carries, it is clear that there can be no happy solution for her. She is being spiritually hunted and there is no escape.

When the real hunt arrives at Hunter's Spinney, the onlookers watch helplessly as the hounds pursue Hazel, fleeing with Foxy in her arms. For her the death pack has arrived and the Black Huntsman, in the form of Reddin, and she falls with Foxy, into the quarry.

''She was gone with Foxy into everlasting silence. She would suck no more honey from the rosy flowers, nor dance like a leaf in the wind. Abel would sit, these next nights, making a small coffin that would leave him plenty of beehive wood."

* * * * * * * * * * *

Soon it became obvious that weekends in Shropshire were simply not enough for Mary who would never be happy away from the land she loved.

* * * * * * * * * * *

Freedom

When on the moss-green hill the wandering wind
Drowses, and lays his brazen trumpet down,
When snow-fed waters gurgle, cold and brown,
And wintered birds creep from the stacks to find
Solace, while each bright eye begins to see
A visionary nest in every tree -
Let us away, out of the murky day
Of sullen towns, into the silver noise
Of woods where every bud has found her way
Sunward, and every leaf has found a voice.

* * * * * * * * * * *

Fortunately Henry was able to secure a job at The Priory School in Shrewsbury and early in 1917 they moved to Lyth Hill. Lyth Hill is just over two miles south west of Shrewsbury and from it you can see almost every range of hills in south Shropshire.

The Webbs moved first into rented accommodation and then bought a piece of land where they built a small cottage. The design of Spring Cottage was Mary's and, from the front door, you can see Caer Caradoc, the Long Mynd and the Devil's Chair.

Here she began work on her third novel "The House in Dormer Forest" - working more slowly than she had ever done before, perhaps because she felt that, at last, she was home. She said herself that she now had the "lovely impossible things I long for ... to live on Lyth Hill and to live in a house of my own."

* * * * * * * * * * *

"The House in Dormer Forest" is set in the countryside near Minsterley, south west of Shrewsbury, at the north end of the Stiperstones. Dormer Valley is actually Hope Valley near Snailbeach.

Not only does landscape play an important role in the novel, but Dormer Old House itself has been described as the most important character. Like Undern Hall in "Gone to Earth", Dormer Old House exerts a powerful and unwholesome influence on those who live in it. And, like Stephen's cottage in "The Golden Arrow", it is burned to the ground once those who gave it life and spirit are no longer there.

The opening of the novel, describing Dormer Old House in the landscape, has been compared with the detailed description of Egdon Heath at the start of Thomas Hardy's novel "The Return of the Native". Both vividly convey a sense of place and a sense of the power landscape exerts over human endeavour.

Mary Webb does not introduce a human character until the second chapter of "The House in Dormer Forest" - an indication of the importance of the house in the plot.

"Dormer Old House stood amid the remnants of primeval woodland that curtained the hills. These rose steeply on all sides of the house, which lay low by the water in the valley."

"...in fine weather, the house and its gardens lay open to the view, small but clear, beside the white thread that was Dormer brook. The place had been patched and enlarged by successive generations, very much as man's ideas are altered, the result in both cases being the same - a mansion to the majority, a prison to the few."

It is not, we are soon aware, a description of a happy house.

"All these things you could see in clear weather, but when it was misty - and mist lingered here as of inalienable right - the house was obliterated. It vanished like a pebble in a well, with all its cabined and shuttered wraths and woes, all its thunderous 'thou shalt nots'. At such times it did not seem that any law ruled in the valley except the law of the white owls and the hasty water and the mazy bat-dances. Only those who slept there night by night could tell you that the house was overspread with a spider's-web of rules, legends and customs so complex as to render the individual soul almost helpless."

The landscape around the house is equally grim and forbidding:

"Round the House of Dormer stood the forest, austerely aloof."

The trees "seemed to peer at the house over one another's shoulders like people looking at something grotesque, not with blame or praise, but in a kind of disdainful indifference."

Against this backdrop the Darke family acts out its drama - that of a younger generation fighting against the repressive narrow-mindedness of the old, which eventually destroys the house.

There are numerous descriptions of Dormer Old House and the surrounding forest and the bitter effect they have on the inhabitants.

Amber Darke, who is probably a self-portrait of the young Mary Webb, struggles constantly to keep her spirit in tact, in spite of her apparently loveless family life and her dismal home.

"Amber looked out into the chill moonlight. On the silver lawn there lay, black and sharp as carved ebony, the shadow of the House of Dormer. Its two heavy, rounded gables of dark red brick topped with grey stone, the solid massed chimneys and the weather-vane ... were painted, large and far-spreading, on the grass. The house gave a sense of solidity even by its shadows."

"As if at the signal of midnight, there now began a new sound, more disturbing and grotesque than the noise of the death-watches - a human stir and murmur, probably started by the sound of the clocks. But the sounds were those of sleep, not of waking life. It was as if the spirits of those in the house, slumbering during the body's activity, half woke, and tried to pierce the silence around them."

"There was something wrong here, (Amber) felt, something sinister and unwholesome. Lost voices came along the tortuous passages, uplifted as if in complaint from amid murky dreams, and as if in baffled longing for some undiscovered good."

Amber lives in Dormer Old House with her parents and maternal grandmother, her brothers Jasper and Peter, her sister Ruby and her cousin Catherine. Peter and Jasper both desire Catherine who, beneath a veneer of religious virtue, is cold-hearted and manipulative.

When Jasper loses his faith, gives up his studies at theological college and becomes a farm hand, Catherine rejects him as an infidel. Thus is she keeping faith with the worn out tenets of the house and the older generation. Peter, also spurned by Catherine, turns to the housemaid Marigold and finds in her, in defiance of his family, an outlet for his suppressed emotions.

Ruby marries a clergyman, not for love but for the sake of some tawdry wedding finery and realises too late that she has condemned herself to a life of unhappiness.

It is Amber, modest and graceful, who finally triumphs over her environment, finding true love in the person of the outsider Michael Hallowes, a friend of Jasper. The calculating but beautiful Catherine tries to steal Michael from her but fails. And Catherine's very ruthlessness proves to be her downfall and she, like Ruby, is trapped into a loveless marriage, with a local farmer.

Over all these dramas preside the terrible figures of the mother Rachel Darke who is loveless and callous, and her mother Hannah who passes harsh judgement on all and sundry, like an Old Testament prophet. It is Hannah who burns Dormer Old House to the ground, freeing all those who have been its prisoners, both spiritually and physically and destroying the awful domination of her daughter Rachel.

There is another character, Enoch the hired servant, through whom Mary Webb expresses her identification with the countryside. He is another in the mould of John Arden in "The Golden Arrow" who is generally believed to be a portrait of her father. Naturally Enoch is sensitive to the mood of the house.

"Enoch was never quite at his ease in Dormer. He liked to be out on the huge purple hills under the towering sky, where the curlews cried out strange news to him in passing, and the little brown doves murmured of a hidden country, a secret law, more limited than those of man, yet more miraculous."

"Anyone who cared to study Enoch came upon a mystery, discovering a being so near the animal world that he could easily interpret the vague half-thoughts of a sheep or a cow, yet so far advanced along the road of psychic development that most other inhabitants of Dormer were pigmies compared with him."

It is only in the house that Enoch feels uneasy. It is not the forest that exerts a malign influence. Although it is a dark and secretive place it has its own beauties - the beauty which Mary Webb always found in nature.

"...the tall beeches and the mountain ash trees, slender and haughty in their flaming scarlet, seemed to give as little heed to the passing of the carriage ... as to the crawling of a brown beetle in the grass, but remained, wrapped in their age-long meditation. Here the road lay beside Dormer brook, which flowed - mute, brown and covert - beneath trees so close and heavy that they plunged the road into green twilight. Tall, early-tinted poplars pricked up, covered with beaten gold, like spires belonging to a worship secret and remote. Sparsely in the hedges grew the pale, infragrant flowers of early autumn - wild snapdragon, scabious, purple and blue wan yarrow and the forlorn harebell.''

Amber, in her loneliness, senses the greatness of the forest and says:

''The forest will sing like this when I am dead. I shall die, but I shall not have lived.''

Although the forest will endure beyond the petty lives of men, the man-made house shows itself coldly indifferent to the fate of its occupants.

''The house watched over its sleeping children careless, it seemed, as to whether they dreamed happily or sadly. If the house stood, what mattered the single soul? ... The house must go on, just as it was, just as it had been for so long. It would go on surely for ever.''

But the forest knows better. The trees:

''Sang of lichens the mosses and elm samaras and rosy seed of pines already preparing for the day when Dormer should be taken back into the earth, curtained in green. For nothing that is built by man for the subjugation of the single soul can stand.''

The other significant place at Dormer is the Beast Walk - as sinister as the house itself and even more surreal.

''The walk, during the whole of its ascent, was bordered on each side by strange beasts and birds cut out of gigantic yew trees. It ended at the grotto which dominated it. Just here the wood was composed of yews and hollies so old that they gave the impression of having existed in the primeval forest.''

The fantastical shapes have been created by generations of Darkes and take many different forms - swans, cattle, sheep, peacocks and a particularly unpleasant monkey. ''All had a nightmare touch'' - reflecting the souls of the Darkes who created them.

Jasper goes to the Beast Walk, tormented by his hopeless love for Catherine, and miserable at his family's harsh treatment of him since his crisis of faith.

''So the Walk had come to symbolise in his mind the Lares and Penates of Dormer, and the beasts were pictures of hoary tradition, prescription, decrepit and unwieldy laws, custom grown senile, a predatory collectivism. ... He felt sometimes as if he had come into a wild beast show and found all the beasts loose. He was realizing that there are depths of savagery in the human heart deeper than that of killing; that when law is put before love and the material before the spiritual there is nothing left wherewith to combat evil; ..."

He realises of those at Dormer that "spiritually they were cannibals".

It is in the Beast Walk that Jasper discovers the truth about Catherine's nature and from there that he runs to drown himself in Dormer brook. Although he does not die, he never returns to live at Dormer Old House.

When the atmosphere of the house oppresses Amber too much, she escapes to the upper woods. Here Mary Webb's delight speaks through her.

"Amber loved to think in winter of the life that ran in the dark tree trunks, of the muffled laughter in every grass-root and crocus bulb; to hear the thrush chanting his prophetic vision of spring far-off in the southern valleys. She loved to watch for the purple and gold and green marvels of elf-land that blossomed out of the dead-black branches; to kneel by the rockery and slip her finger into a corolla of the blue gentian, where it was warmer than the outer air."

It is amidst the glories of nature that bestow on Amber a beauty greater than that of her physical self, that Michael Hallowes first comes across her.

"So it came to pass that he surprised the very self of Amber Darke abroad in the blue day, hovering like a bee in the foam of flowers."

"They looked at one another, and their look was that of friends who have met a long while since, in other lands, to the sound of wilder music, but with the same remembered ecstasy."

It is inevitable that they will marry in spite of the worst that Catherine can do, and appropriately, theirs is a forest bridal. They walk home through a woodland of almost supernatural beauty as Mary Webb unravels scene after scene of acutely observed description of the colour and forms of nature.

"Amber thought of June mornings when polished birds with flaming yellow bills made large tracks in the dew-white grass. She thought of the subtle changes of the seasons, breathlessly fair, not one to be spared. She remembered dawns that bloomed like a hedge of roses above the amethyst hills, and the bank of white violets which had never missed her yet in April. These things were her home, not Dormer.''

In the final chapter Dormer Old House burns to the ground, mourned by noone except perhaps Rachel Darke who sees with its destruction, the passing of her power. And the forest all around, continues unchanged.

''From its height the forest contemplated them. It had its own preoccupations, its dreams of bronze and copper and clear gold. It was cold to the death of humans and of houses.''

* * * * * * * * * * *

''The House in Dormer Forest'' was published two years after the end of the war, in 1920. For the first time several publishers were interested in taking it, and Mary received better payment than ever before, for both this and her next novel.

In spite of this and the fact that the war was over, Mary was listless and depressed. Always sensitive about her appearance, she became extremely jealous of Henry who found it increasingly difficult to sustain normal social relationships, especially with women.

Both Henry and their doctor believed that a change of scene would be of benefit to Mary and in January 1921 the Webbs moved to a furnished flat in Hampstead, London, Henry having obtained a suitable teaching post. After a few months they moved to a tiny cottage, still in Hampstead.

Knowing Mary's feelings about Shropshire and her unhappiness both in Weston-super-Mare and Chester, it seems clear that the experiment was doomed to failure. But she had hopes that living in London might enable her to meet and form contacts with people in the literary world. She must have hoped that she might at last receive some of the critical acclaim that was by this time, her due. Sadly, she was to be disappointed.

* * * * * * * * * * *

On Receiving a Box of Spring Flowers in London
So the old, dear freemasonry goes on -
The busy life, the laughter-under-sod,
The leafy hosts with spear and gonfalon
Guarding the earthy mysteries of God.

I did not think the violets came so soon,
Yet here are five, and all my room is sweet;
And here's an aconite - a golden moon
Shining where all her raying leaflets meet;

And here's a snowdrop, finely veined - ah, see!
Fresh from the artist's hand, and folded close:
She only waits the sunshine and the bee;
Then she will open like a golden rose.

* * * * * * * * * * *

Mary Webb wrote about London only twice in her fiction, in two short stories, "Palm" and "In Affection and Esteem", both of which describe women suffering because of the conditions in which they are forced to live.

In "In Affection and Esteem" Myrtle Brown, who earns a meagre living stitching buttonholes in a London shop, dreams of being sent bunches of flowers. She longs to arrive home one night to find her room full of blossom.

"The little room would be like a greenhouse - like one of the beautiful greenhouses at Kew - with the passionate purity of tall lilies; with pansies softly creased; with cowslips in tight bunches, and primroses edged with dark leaves, and daffodils with immense frail cups. She would borrow jam-pots from the landlady, and it would take all evening to arrange them. And the room would be wonderful - like heaven. The flowers would pour out incense, defeating the mustiness of the house and the permanent faint scent of cabbage."

In Myrtle Brown's longing, one senses Mary Webb's own sentiments at being stuck in the city, so far away from all that she loved. London cannot be portrayed as anything other than a grey prison, a place in which to dream and endure until the opportunity to escape should arise.

* * * * * * * * * * *

The Webbs returned to Spring Cottage for Easter 1921 and Mary decided to stay there to continue with a new novel which she had started in Hampstead. Henry visited at weekends but found Mary feeling lonely and still depressed. Eventually she returned to London and began to write reviews for The Spectator and The Bookman. She also wrote short stories, some of which were published in The

English Review. During this time Mary did meet well-known literary figures such as Walter de la Mare who included some of her poems in his anthology "Come Hither".

But altogether it was an unhappy restless period for Mary - lonely away from Henry but miserable away from Shropshire. And it was in these difficult circumstances, when writing cannot have been easy for her, that Mary Webb completed her fourth novel, "Seven for a Secret."

* * * * * * * * * * *

To a Blackbird Singing in London

Sing on, dear bird! Bring the old rapturous pain,
In this great town, where I no welcome find.
Show me the murmuring forest in your mind,
And April's fragile cups, brimful of rain.
O sing me far away, that I may hear
The voice of grass, and, weeping, may be blind
To slights and lies and friends that prove unkind,
Sing till my soul dissolves into a tear,
Glimmering within a chaliced daffodil.
So, when the stately sun with burning breath
Absorbs my being, I'll dream that he is Death,
Great Death, the undisdainful. By his will
No more unlovely, haunting all things fair,
I'll seek some kinder life in the golden air.

* * * * * * * * * * *

"Seven for a Secret" is set in the Clun Forest area of south west Shropshire, which Mary Webb names Dysgwlfas-on-the-Wild-Moors. It is not generally considered to be one of her best novels although Robert Lynd wrote: "a tempestuous energy storms through the landscape of (the book)." And it is true that, although in common with her other novels, there is not a great deal of action in it, "Seven for a Secret" gives an impression of busyness.

The novel opens with a description of landscape and buildings rather than of people.

"On a certain cold winter evening, in the country that lies between the dimpled lands of England and the gaunt purple steeps of

Wales - half in Faery and half out of it - the old farm-house that stood in the midst of the folds and billows of Dysgwlfas-on-the-Wild-Moors glowed with a deep gem-like lustre in its vast setting of grey and violet. Moorland country is never colourless. It still keeps, when every heather-bell is withered, in its large mysterious expanses, a bloom of purple like the spirit of the heather."

This farmhouse is the home of Gillian Lovekin, a slightly unusual heroine for Mary Webb as she is flighty, superficial and thoughtless, although possessing a certain physical beauty. The two men who desire her represent the two aspects of love - a theme explored again and again in Mary Webb's fiction.

Ralph Elmer is a character like Jack Reddin. A ruthless new-comer to Dysgwlfas, he represents profane love, while the farmhand Robert Rideout who is sensitive and loyal, represents sacred love. Early on, we are given glimpses of Robert's character.

"Robert was as simple, as unselfconscious as a child, without a child's egotism. He saw the landscape, not Robert Rideout in the landscape. He saw the sheep, not Robert Rideout as the kindly shepherd in the midst of the sheep. Mountains did not make him think of himself climbing. He did not, as nine hundred and ninety-nine people out of every hundred do, instinctively look at himself when he came to a pond."

He is of the land, almost a part of it, and as with the land, Gillian scarcely notices him, until it is too late. She craves excitement and adventure, her ultimate ambition being to go to London. To this end she persuades her Aunt to invite her to stay in Silverton, (based on Shrewsbury) seeing this as the first step to London.

Gillian, in her immaturity, finds the moors lonely, while Robert Rideout, because he is receptive to nature, cannot live away from them - they are in his blood.

"Day after day, in the early morning or after his work was done, he brooded upon the waste as it lay beneath his gaze, self-wrapped, conning its own secret, dreaming of itself and its dark history, its purple-mantled past and its future clothed in vaporous mystery. The colour that comes on the heather when it is in full flower, which is like the bloom on a plum, was in his dream."

"Far beyond the rim of blue was still the moorland - the secret moorland, with its savage peace. There the curlews cried, eerie and lonely, in spring. Thence the wind drew, urgent, vital. And always, whether he was at market or chapel, in the farm or the inn, which lay alone out on the moor, he heard - whatever the weather or the season - as it were a long way off, and far down in his consciousness - the roar of the winter wind over the bleak, snowy acres of Dysgwlfas."

"There was something waiting for him there in the future - some deed, some high resolve. Was it death? It was mysterious as death, he thought. All his days he walked in this dream, which did not hinder his deft hands nor his quick feet, and continually the country spun more threads between itself and him."

Gillian gets her wish and Robert drives her on the cart to catch the train to Silverton, at Mallard's Keep, Mary Webb's name for Bishops Castle.

"There it shone, its clustered roofs, square church tower and miniature railway station all sloping up a hill with the inconsequence of a card house. Beyond were meadows, steep woods, blue distance, smoke-coloured hills, and more hills so pale as to fade on the sky."

By this time Robert is in love with Gillian although she thinks nothing of him. He does not want her to go to Silverton but he cannot follow her. He is bound in some, as yet mysterious way, to the land.

"The road twisted back for a few yards, and they faced towards Dysgwlfas... There was his home. There he must bide until he had fulfilled his task, silently laid upon him by the silent moor. He must drag its heart out, mingle it with his own being, make it into something lovely and unfading. The soul of Gillian Lovekin should also be mingled with it. He had no knowledge, no words, no books, yet he would do it."

He is prepared to say goodbye to Gillian at Mallard's Keep but she pulls him onto the train, in order that he should have tea with her at The Junction (Craven Arms) while she waits for her connection to Silverton. He is angry because he senses that she is playing games with him but by the time they reach The Junction "past the three wayside stations set in the woods" his good-humour is restored and they have tea in the "one tea-shop in the single street".

Gillian then continues her journey to Silverton alone.

"The country grew dimmer, grew dark, in the short journey... Once she saw the far hills dark against the afterglow, once she caught a glimpse of a brook lit by reflected radiance. Then came straggling houses, a village church, houses clustering thicker, roofs all huddled together, a square church tower, two silver spires, a great bridge across the Severn - Silverton.''

Ralph Elmer comes to Dysgwlfas while Gillian is away in Silverton. He moves into the recently vacated inn The Mermaid's Rest, near which is a stretch of land known as ''the unket place''.

''A flash of water at its foot, a flash of bright moss-green on its side, a dreaming yellow in its larch boughs where the knops were swelling towards the leaves - why, then, was it so grievous? It must be what he (Robert) had said to Gillian: evil had broken through there, or would - a horror, strong and fierce as some great beast, would split the solid earth and raven through the land. And again, like a warning bell, came the intuition that he would see it happen, that he must wrestle with something stupendous, even here at the gates of home.''

It is Robert who first brings Ralph Elmer to The Mermaid's Rest and the unket place.

''... Ralph turned to the surrounding country, and his gaze travelled over it. There, lower than the inn, one field away from the browny-white ribbon of road, lay the unket place - ... He stiffened a little, like a dog at a new scent, pricked his ears slightly, stared. And out of nowhere, like the faint lament of a sheep from cloudy heights, came the knowledge that this place was prepared for him, had always been waiting for him, quietly and unobtrusively, and would not let him go until what must be had been accomplished.''

So the stage is set for the climactic events which are to take place there. Events which are as inevitable as they are, thus far, mysterious.

When Gillian returns she falls in love with Elmer, as Robert feared she would. Just as Silverton did, Elmer represents excitement and passion. She believes that she will never be bored with him.

''So she remained in love with passion, and Elmer was its exponent. Strange glories, strange despairs and wonders dazzled her through the wild, chilly April days. For at Dysgwlfas April is as cold as a snowflake. No blossom comes upon the trees, no pale light of primroses lies along the sparse woods until May.''

''And through all these spring days, in the strangest and most mysterious way, invisible threads spun themselves between the Unket Place and four very different people.''

Gillian, Ralph Elmer, Robert Rideout and Rwth, Elmer's dumb

servant girl - these four will be the protagonists in the final drama of the unket place.

"... it was as though, in silence and in patience, invisible hands began to prepare a stage for some drama."

The drama is set in motion when Gillian goes to the fair at Weeping Cross (Knighton) with Elmer, even though, deep inside, she is beginning to realise that she would rather be with Robert.

"Then they saw a long way off, in a veil of rain, the small shining steeple, the low shining roofs - red and brown and blue - the clustered trees, half in leaf, the nestling ricks, the apple-green fields of Weeping Cross... It was a place she would have most liked to see with Robert; but as she could not, she liked almost as much to see it with Elmer."

At Weeping Cross Elmer seduces Gillian and the following morning she wakes to the awful realisation that it is Robert she loves. But when Robert and her father arrive, she pretends that she loves Elmer knowing that otherwise Robert would kill him, and then hang. Elmer is coerced into marriage with Gillian even though he is already married to Rwth, a secret known only to his blackmailing servant Fringal.

On the night before the wedding, at The Mermaid's Rest, we are reminded that it is nature that ultimately triumphs over the greatest efforts of man.

"... in the hush of night, the house wove minute sounds - the gnawing of a rat in an empty room; the rustling of a bat's wings in the passage; the faint rasping of the feet of a daddy-long-legs, advancing upon Fringal with its extraordinary ghoulish clownishness; the hoot of an owl in the unket place; and the everlasting whisper of the moor which changed into a roar in winter, but never died, and which was, even at its quietest, like the lisp of one destined to become a conqueror."

- a description reminiscent of the equally restless Dormer Old House at night.

In time Robert begins to suspect the truth about Rwth and persuades the unsuspecting Gillian to teach her to write, so that she will be able to communicate the awful injustices inflicted on her by Elmer. Because he has been led to believe that Gillian loves Elmer, his suspicions bring no joy to Robert. Unselfishly, although he believes he has lost her to a man he dislikes, he wants her happiness more than revenge. His own refuge he seeks in the moors.

"He wrapped himself in the moor, and he attained a beauty he could not have won in a town. Little by little he made his poem - rugged, sweet and wild - and when he sat alone by the fire in the evenings, he was comforted by this unifying of himself with the beauty of the earth, by this caging and taming of remote loveliness, by the welding of phrases and the ripple of metres and the mysterious mingling of his soul with the sweeping dark expanses with their grey roofing cloud. And the vast moor, seamed and chasmed with streams, the immense heaven, veiled and feathered with cloud were like his own personality - large and vital, passionate and stormy, yet veined with melancholy and brooded over by philosophy."

But he cannot escape the malign influence of the unket place, knowing that his destiny is bound up with it, and that he is to be involved in some great struggle for Gillian's sake, although he does not know what form it will take.

"And Robert, glancing at the Unket Place as he led away his flock, knew that the hour was coming soon when his presage would be fulfilled, when evil would leap out and there would be none to wrestle with it but himself..."

Rwth eventually reveals in writing, the secret of her abduction from her parents and subsequent forced marriage to Elmer. Later Elmer comes across her gathering wood in the unket place.

"As he stood there, that which Robert had so long forseen came to pass. From somewhere, from nowhere, out of the earth or the pallid sky, or out of Fringal's bleak mind, burst the spirit of evil. It tore through the shreds and patches of good in Ralph Elmer; it laid hold of the kindness in him with tooth and claw, and rent it..."

"He lifted the gun to his shoulder and fired. Rwth fell forward without a sound. She slipped into eternity within the globing peace of her love, as the chrysalis of a dragon-fly might go down-stream in a water-lily. Certainly to her the Unket Place had not been unket, but kind."

Inevitably Robert discovers Elmer's crime but prepares to take the blame upon himself, still believing that Gillian loves him. Thus is he willing to make the ultimate sacrifice and die for the sake of Gillian's happiness. She however, discovers his intention, learns the truth, and the two are united at last.

* * * * * * * * * * *

MARY WEBB IN HER FINAL YEARS

Mary Webb completed "Seven for a Secret" towards the end of 1921 and asked Thomas Hardy's permission to dedicate it to him.

By this time, although critics were generally approving of her work, her books were still not a commercial success. None of her books had sold more than one thousand copies. Added to this disappointment was the fact that she was in virtually permanent ill-health and was giving away most of the little money she had, to those she believed to be more in need than herself.

In spite of these drawbacks Mary Webb was still to write her most famous novel "Precious Bane". The plot was drafted at Spring Cottage but most of the book was written at Hampstead.

* * * * * * * * * * *

"Precious Bane" tells the story of Prue Sarn, a young woman who's looks are marred by a hare-lip. Local people believe that this affliction is the result of a hare having crossed her mother's path when she was pregnant. Thus it amounts almost to a curse.

"... it was a curse that ... the hare gave me. I wondered why it cursed me so. Was it of its own free will and wish, or did the devil drive it? Did God begrutch me an 'usband and a cot of rushes, that He'd let it be so?... And I knew it would take a deal of money to cure a hare-shotten lip. There was a kind of sour laughter in the thought of it. It called to mind the blackish autumn evenings, when grouse rise from the bitter marsh and fly betwixt the withered heather and the freezing sky, and laugh."

And, in spite of the transparent beauty of her nature, Prue is regarded with suspicion by superstitious people and believed by some to be a witch.

"For they'd even begun to say of me that I took shape as a hare on dark moonless nights, and went loping across the hills, and had a muse running under the churchyard. Such things were first said in idleness or mischief or to scare children, and then, in the loneliness of old farms, full of creakings and moanings on windy nights, they grew. And none can tell what such things will grow into at long last, nor what harm they may do."

By giving her heroine a physical deformity, Mary Webb was writing about herself and her distress at her own appearance, marred as it was by the effects of Graves Disease.

Prue falls in love with the weaver Kester Woodseaves but believes that, as soon as he sees her clearly, any chance of his returning her love will disappear. But Kester sees beyond Prue's deformity and loves her for her sweet nature and strong spirit, taking care also to draw attention to her physical assets - her trim figure and her melting dark eyes.

This ignoring of, or looking beyond physical defects is a theme which occurred in Mary Webb's earlier novels, although in less graphic terms. Amber Darke is not a beautiful woman but Michael Hallowes scarcely sees her face at all - only her inner beauty. And when Robert Rideout claims Gillian Lovekin, the scar on her forehead seems to disappear. This was Mary Webb writing out her own dearest wish.

There is some disagreement about the precise location of Sarn Mere, the lake which broods alongside Prue and Gideon's farmhouse. Some sources identify it as Ellesmere, in the far north of Shropshire and others as Bomere Pool, south of Shrewsbury. The most likely answer is that given by Mary Webb's biographer Gladys Mary Coles, who believes that Sarn Mere is made up of elements taken from several locations - Ellesmere, Colemere, Bomere Pool and Shomere Pool.

The atmosphere particularly may have been drawn from Bomere Pool which has many strange tales and legends connected with it. It once had a Roman city on its shores and, in the fifteenth century, was a place of pilgrimage. Prue describes the atmosphere of Sarn Mere:

"... there's a discouragement about the place. It may be the water lapping, year in and year out - everywhere you look and listen, water; or the big trees waiting and considering on your right hand and on your left; or the unbreathing quiet of the place, as if it was created but an hour gone, and not created for us."

As an old woman, telling this her story, she says:

"When I look out of my window and see the plain and the big sky with clouds standing up on the mountains, I call to mind the thick, blotting woods of Sarn, and the crying of the mere when the ice was on it... There was but little sky to see there, saving that which was reflected in the mere; but the sky that is in the mere is not the proper heavens. You see it in a glass darkly, and the long shadows of rushes go thin and sharp across the sliding stars, and even the sun and moon might be put out down there, for, times, the moon would get lost in lily leaves, and, times, a heron might stand before the sun."

And Gideon Sarn has cold grey eyes, like the mere in winter.

After the death of his father, Gideon, driven by greed for money and power, works himself, Prue and their mother like slaves, in order to build up the farm and make it prosper. Prue finds her only place of refuge in the attic where the apples are stored. Here, while she practises writing, the spiritual side of her nature blossoms.

"I fell to thinking how all this blessedness of the attic came through me being curst. For if I hadna had a hare-lip to frighten me away into my own lonesome soul, this would never have come to me. The apples would have crowded all in vain to see a marvel, for I should never have known the glory that came from the other side of silence.

"Even while I was thinking this, out of nowhere suddenly came that lovely thing, and nestled in my heart, like a seed from the core of love."

Prue and Gideon go regularly to the market in Lullingford to sell their wares. Gladys Mary Coles identifies this town as Ludlow, on the southern border of the county.

"There was one broad street of black and white houses, jutting out above, and gabled, and made into rounded shop windows below. They stood back in little gardens. At the top of the street was the church, long and low, with a tremendous high steeple, well carved and pleasant to see. Under the shadow of the church was the big, comfortable inn, with its red sign painted with a tall blue mug of cider."

The town provides a sharp contrast with Sarn.

"For there was summat about Lullingford, as if a different air blew there, and a safer daylight. I knew not why it was."

And, it is the home of Kester Woodseaves, who's house is as attractive to Prue as Sarn is dismal and sad.

Mary Webb loved selling her own produce in Shrewsbury market and she draws on her detailed knowledge of market life in this novel.

"The market was in the open, in a paven square by the church. Each had his own booth, and the cheeses stood in mounds between. There were a sight of old women in decent shawls and cotton bonnets selling the same as we had; butter and eggs and poultry. There was a stall for gingerbread and one for mincepies. There was a sunbonnet stall and a toy stall, and one for gewgaws such as strings of coral and china cats, shoe buckles and amulets and beaded reticules.

It was a merry scene, with the bright holly and the mistletoe, the cheeses yellow in the sun, and the gingerbread as brown and sticky as chestnut buds."

Even Gideon is affected by "holiday feeling" and tells Prue of his plans to make them rich.

"But Gideon wanted to talk while the holiday feeling was on him, afore the dumbness of Sarn got the better of him agen. For it was a most peculiar thing how you couldna speak your heart out at Sarn, and I never knew whether it was the big trees brooding, or the heavy rheumaticky feeling of being so close to the water or the ancient house full of the remembrances of old ancient people, or that there was summat forboded."

Gideon is doomed to bring destruction on himself and those close to him because of his single-minded obsession with acquiring wealth. Although he is in love with Jancis Beguildy, the wizard's daughter, he refuses to marry her until his finances will, as he sees it, support a wife and child, without jeopardising his plans. In the interim Jancis is obliged to hire herself out for three years as a maid on a distant farm, where she is so miserable that she runs away and throws herself on the mercy of Prue and Gideon.

Although he forgives Jancis the great sin of forfeiting her wages, Gideon still refuses to marry her but becomes instead her lover. Her father Wizard Beguildy, already set against the match, takes revenge on Gideon by setting fire to his newly harvested crops, destroying them all. A kind of madness takes hold of Gideon as all his hopes are consumed before his eyes and he rejects Jancis completely even though she is now carrying his child. Even after its birth he is unrelenting and Jancis drowns herself and the child in Sarn Mere.

Throughout "Precious Bane" the mood of the various stages of the plot seems to be reflected in the mood of the countryside which Prue describes in different seasons.

Spring is a time of hope and Prue's thoughts turn to Kester.

"Yet as I thought of Kester Woodseaves and what he had come to mean, I seemed to hear and see, on this side and on that, in the dark woods, a sound and gleam of the gathering of spring. There was a piping call in the oak wood, a bursting of purple in the tree-tops, a soft yellowing of celandine in the rookery. When I was come into the attic, spring was there afore me, though it was so cold that my hands could scarce write. None the less, I put down in my book the words, 'The first day of spring'."

And even the grinding drudgery of farm work seems less awful.

"When April came we were still ploughing, and I was so used to it that I'd given over being tired, and enjoyed it, and sang to myself the while. It was grand to go down the red furrow with the share cutting strong into the stiff earth and shining like silver. It was fine to look away to the blue hills by Lullingford, and see the woods of oak and larch and willow all in bud between, as if a warm wind blew from there and called the leaves."

Kester's voice is like summer-time.

"It was like a wide, blossomy thorn-tree on a sweltering day in early June. You could sit down under it and rest you."

But, Jancis in her frailty, both of body and mind, is doomed.

"And whenever I thought of Jancis I called to mind a thing I saw once in June, when we had strange untoert weather and a deal of tempest and sleat, which one day for about an hour turned to snow. And I saw the wild rose so tender and nesh, and used to nothing colder than dew, with their pale pink petals all full of snow, and seeming to be frozen through and through, gold hearts and all."

And, when she runs away from Grimble's farm and comes to Sarn, it is in the dead of winter.

"The trees were mounded up with snow, and the mere frozen till near the middle. The woods, as white as sugar, stood round the water so still, as if they were spelled, like folk in some old tale of witchcraft, so deep they were in trusses and bales of snow, and not a breath stirring. You couldna call summer to mind."

"There against the white, dreary stretch of the frozen mere, all wobegone and white in the light of the fire, was Jancis."

She is forgiven and summer comes again, a happy time when the corn is growing and the mere loses its threat.

"That was the best time of year for our lake, when in the still, hot noons the water looked so kind, being of a calm, pale blue, that you would never think it could drown anybody. All round stood the tall trees, thick-leaved with rich summer green, unstirring, caught in a spell, sending down their coloured shadows into the mere, so that the tree-tops almost met in the middle."

"For though Sarn was an ill place to live, and in the wintry months a very mournful place, at this one time of the year it left dreaming of sorrow and was as other fair stretches of wood and water."

Prue revels in the beauty of the waterlilies and the numerous species of dragonfly on the mere.

"Within the ring of rushes was another ring of lilies, and at this time of year they were the most beautiful thing at Sarn, and the most beautiful thing I'd ever seen. The big bright leaves lay calm upon the water, and calmer yet upon the leaves, lay the lilies, white and yellow. When they were buds, they were like white and gold birds sleeping, head under wing, or like summat carven out of glistering stone, or, as I said afore, they were like gouts of pale wax. But when they were come into full blow they wunna like anything but themselves, and they were so lovely you couldna choose but cry to see them."

"There were plenty of dragon-flies about, both big and little. There were the big blue ones that are so strong they will fly over top of the tallest tree if you fritten them, and there were the tiny thin ones that seem almost too small to be called dragon-flies at all. There were rich blue kingfisher-flies and those we called damsels, coloured and polished in the manner of lustre ware. There were a good few with clear wings of no colour or of faint green, and a tuthree with a powdery look like you see on the leaves of 'rickluses. Some were tawny like a fitchet cat, some were rusty or coloured like the copper fruit-kettle. Jewels, they made you think of, precious gems such as be listed in the Bible."

Down by the mere in summer Prue gets to know Kester and realises with joy that her deformity means nothing to him.

But when Gideon takes the dangerous step of becoming Jancis' lover, there is a hint of autumn sorrow in the air.

"... off he went, whistling loud and clear, up the wood path where the leaves were turning rusty, and sighs were sounding here and there, and the airs breathing autumn, and the brown cobs falling with little thuds,..."

"Why was it so sad, I wondered, when the wedding was fixed so soon, and the glory roses blooming, corn safe housed, and in my own heart the Maister come? Yet there was that about the evening which you feel when summat has died."

And the hint of sorrow to come turns into reality when the harvest is fired and all their labour wasted. After the fire, not only does Gideon reject Jancis, he also murders Mrs Sarn because she has become an invalid and is no longer of any use on the farm. When Prue challenges him, he makes no attempt to deny it.

"Calm? Oh, he was calm as the mere when it was frozen deep."

The even greater catastrophe of Jancis' death follows and the mere has claimed its first victims. Then, Gideon begins to see Jancis in visions.

"Over the mere a mist was rising, in trails and wisps, white as wool, thickening and gathering into clotted heaps towards the mid of the mere. Sometimes a wreath of mist would be drawn out like a scarf, and other times it would stand up in the shape of a woman, but wavering upon the air."

Gradually his feelings of guilty fear grow stronger and Sarn becomes more and more desolate.

"The sounds in the room were less than on the evening Father died. It was as if Sarn, all the live part of it, us and our beasts, the trees full of birds, and the wood ways with wild creatures in them, had sunk to the bottom of the mere where the village was."

Finally, inevitably, Gideon follows Jancis and his child into the mere.

"... the water was his grave. Ah! The whole of that great stretch of water wasna too much to make the grave of a man as strong as that one. The mile-long mist that lay upon the place wasna too grand a shroud. For though he was wrong, and did evil, and hurted folk with his strength, yet he never did meanly, nor turned out bad work, nor lied."

On the morning after Gideon's death the mere has changed, as if a spell has been broken.

"As soon as the mist lifted, I saw that the mere had broken in the night, and the water was thick and troubled, simmering all over, so that the lilies were stirred as they lay anchored. When the blessed sunshine came, a way out came also into my mind. It was fair day."

Prue leaves Sarn forever, stopping only to sell off the livestock. The local people, already believing her to be a witch, turn against her, blaming her for the deaths at Sarn. They inflict on her the traditional punishment for witches, the ducking-stool, but she is saved from a worse fate by the arrival of Kester.

"He stooped. He set his arms about me. He lifted me to the saddle. It was just as in the dream I had." And, in a longed for but scarcely hoped for gesture, "he bent his comely head and kissed me full on the mouth."

* * * * * * * * * * *

''Precious Bane'' was Mary Webb's last complete novel and is considered by many people to be her finest, a culmination of her artistic and spiritual endeavours. It was published in July 1924 but received a lukewarm reception from the critics.

However in the spring of 1925 Mary Webb was awarded the ''Femina Vie Heureuse Award'' for ''Precious Bane''. This award was made for the best fictional work of poetry or prose, representative of English life, by a relatively unknown author.

In the same year Mary's mother died and she attended the funeral in Chester. The two women had kept in touch, in spite of the fact that their relationship had not always been a happy one, and her mother had visited Spring Cottage several times.

At about this time Mary's own health began to deteriorate rapidly. Not only was she suffering from the frustration of poor sales of her novels and increasing debts but also the, partial at least, breakdown of her marriage.

In early 1926 she began to write another novel ''Armour Wherein He Trusted'' but progress was slow and difficult. She was obsessively jealous of her husband and violent swings in her mood meant that she went for long periods without writing at all.

One bright spot in all this misery was a letter she received in January 1927. It was from the then Prime Minister, Stanley Baldwin, who praised ''Precious Bane'' in glowing terms. Mary replied to his letter, describing her new novel and making him a gift of violets for his desk.

But, although in her letter Mary talked of publishing her new novel in the spring, it was actually barely half-written. Soon afterwards she attempted to destroy the manuscript on the fire but Henry rescued it, fortuitiously, as she had instantly regretted her hasty action. She was however to add little more to it and it was published after her death as a fragment, along with ten short stories.

* * * * * * * * * * *

''Armour Wherein He Trusted'' differs from Mary Webb's other novels in that it is set in an earlier period of history, the eleventh century, just after the Norman Conquest. But, like her other novels, the theme is the constant conflict between the flesh and the spirit, although it has more of an air of myth or legend, than of a straightforward country story. The setting is identifiable as the Welsh borderland but the landscape is often stylised, almost heraldic.

"Coming out of the garden in the dusk, I saw the forest stand up like a dim curtain of Bayeux, with here a vasty oak and there a clump of ellums, and every burgeoning tump of trees was like the boss of a shield, so that it seemed some lady had embroidered this curtain with the bossed shields of a great army."

Alongside these are her usual vivid descriptions of existing places.

"Down gentle hillsides, clad in the blackness of pines, came runlets and rivers of white. In bosky places beside the water it lay like curdled milk. And in such places as Long Mountain, where they had ploughed linches along the hillsides, every linch had its scattered sentinels of thorn; in those underhill clearings where a gore acre ran up to a point in the woodland it was prinked out in white like the ermine on a lady's gown. I mind how at Pontesford above the mill was a great may-tree like the mercy of God, spread everywise, and doubled in the pool. I stopped there, letting my beast drink, and gathering a bunch of may for my hat, looking into the wonder of the whey-coloured blossoms with their centres of the rich rose of sword-tassels."

The hero of the tale is Gilbert of Polrebec (Castle Pulverbatch) who is first seen riding in the woods.

"So I riding alone in the oak woods, wending towards Powis (Which as all men know is in the Marches of Wales, a savage country in part, but quieter in Sciropshire and ruled and misruled by the Lords Marchers) a young knight in my hey-day..."

He meets and falls in love with Nesta - a love which is doomed because she is descended from Merlin and has fairy blood. When Gilbert asks where she comes from:

"'Sir', she made answer, 'it lies betwixt Salop and Radnor. It lies also between life and death. It is betwixt and between all things'."

When Gilbert is with Nesta his world becomes less prosaic and more fantastical.

"So we rode away into a world of dreams, and the dreaming mistletoe still hung there, green gold, the oaks still called ancient things to mind, and the thorn that I found budded was white over."

But as a Christian Gilbert is mistaken in believing that he can find happiness with Nesta, even though he ignores all warning signs and marries her.

"'Why, by your looks, you might be an elf maid, feared of all Christian things!' I cried."

Gilbert takes Nesta home to Polrebec to live with him, his parents and his aunt. We learn that his father lives with him because his own castle of Stretton-in-the-Dale is surrounded by enemies.

There follows a period of calm when Nesta appears to settle into the household. Gilbert, as he works the farm, describes the landscape of the Stiperstones and the Long Mynd.

"Now I was up on Long-mynd, looking for estrays afore light on a dewy May morning ... I turned west, where, in the light of coming dawn, I could see Breidden, that lordly twinned mountain, standing sharp and dark on the silver of eternity. There was Powis, and my love sleeping..."

"I turned my back on Powis and looked beyond Caradoc to the rim of plain and the sky lightened as if one lifted a lanthorn out of sight."

All this time the sense of God is very strong in Gilbert and when Peter the Hermit sends for him to go on the First Crusade to the Holy Land, there is no doubt that he will obey, reluctant though he is to leave his family.

This is almost the end of the fragment. The last few pages give an indication that all is not well with Nesta at Polrebec, when Gilbert is no longer there, but Mary Webb's plans for the rest of the novel can only be guessed at.

* * * * * * * * * * *

In 1927 Mary Webb returned to Shropshire and, in the summer, did her final piece of writing which was a review of a novel by Edith Wharton. She spent most of her time alone and was suffering from the after-effects of shock from a fall in the house in Hampstead.

Henry did visit her during the summer but had to return to London for the new school term in September, and Mary followed him. By this time her condition was extremely serious and, deciding that a complete rest was necessary, she arranged to visit her old friend Miss Lory at St Leonards on Sea in Sussex.

Miss Lory was so alarmed at Mary's condition when she arrived on the train that she took her straight to a nursing home where, two days later, on October 18th 1927, she died. She was forty-six. The cause of death was given as pernicious anaemia and Graves Disease.

* * * * * * * * * * *

Safe
Under a blossoming tree
Let me lie down,
With one blackbird to sing to me
In the evenings brown.
Safe from the world's long importunity -
The endless talk, the critical, sly stare,
The trifling social days - and unaware
Of all the bitter thoughts they have of me,
Low in the grass, deep in the daisies,
I shall sleep sound, safe from their blames and praises.

* * * * * * * * * * *

Ironically, only a few months later, Stanley Baldwin praised ''Precious Bane'' at a literary dinner and, almost overnight, Mary Webb became a bestseller. It was her virtually estranged husband and his new wife who benefitted from her posthumous success.

Although her books have enjoyed reasonable popularity since her death, sadly, only two novels, ''Gone to Earth'' and ''Precious Bane'' and a selection of her poetry are still in print, although at the time of writing I understand that there are plans afoot to produce a new edition of all her novels and a collected edition of her poems.

Brief Bibliography

W. R. Chappell - The Shropshire of Mary Webb (Cecil Palmer 1930)

Gladys Mary Coles - The Flower of Light (Duckworth 1978)

Thomas Moult - Mary Webb: her life and work (Cape 1932)

Michael Raven - A Shropshire Gazetteer (Raven 1989)

Vincent Waite - Shropshire Hill Country (Dent 1970)

Dorothy P. H. Wrenn - Goodbye to Morning (Shrewsbury, Wildings 1964)

But chiefly, Mary Webb's own writing.